W9-ARJ-724

The Chumash
and Their History

by Natalie M. Rosinsky

Content Adviser: Bruce Bernstein, Ph.D.,
Assistant Director for Cultural Resources,
National Museum of the American Indian, Smithsonian Institution

Reading Adviser: Rosemary G. Palmer, Ph.D.,
Department of Literacy, College of Education,
Boise State University

SOUTH HUNTINGTON
PUBLIC LIBRARY
HUNTINGTON STATION, NY 11746

COMPASS POINT BOOKS
MINNEAPOLIS, MINNESOTA

J 970.3
Rosinsky

Compass Point Books
3109 West 50th Street, #115
Minneapolis, MN 55410

Visit Compass Point Books on the Internet at *www.compasspointbooks.com*
or e-mail your request to *custserv@compasspointbooks.com*

On the cover: Detail from a mural of tomol paddlers at the Channel Islands
National Marine Sanctuary

Photographs ©: Photos Courtesy of Robert V. Schwemmer, the Maritime Heritage Coordinator for the Channel
Islands National Marine Sanctuary, cover, 16, 38; Prints Old & Rare, back cover (far left); Library of
Congress, back cover; NASA, 4; Marilyn "Angel" Wynn, 5, 8, 11, 13, 14, 15, 17, 20, 21, 22, 24, 37, 39; The
Granger Collection, New York, 7; David Muench/Corbis, 9; Courtesy of The Bancroft Library, University of
California, Berkeley, 18; Craig Aurness/Corbis, 25; Carol Moss/Morro Bay State Park Museum of Natural
History, 27; North Wind Picture Archives, 28, 30, 32, 33, 35; Visuals Unlimited/D. Cunningham, 29;
California Historical Society, 34; Ralph A. Clevenger/Corbis, 41; John Cross/The Free Press, 48.

Creative Director: Terri Foley
Managing Editor: Catherine Neitge
Art Director: Keith Griffin
Photo Researcher: Marcie C. Spence
Designer/Page production: Bradfordesign, Inc./Les Tranby
Cartographer: XNR Productions, Inc.

Library of Congress Cataloging-in-Publication Data
Rosinsky, Natalie M. (Natalie Myra)
    The Chumash and their history / by Natalie M. Rosinsky.
        p. cm.—(We the people)
    Includes bibliographical references and index.
    ISBN 0-7565-0835-5 (hardcover)
1. Chumash Indians—History—Juvenile literature. 2. Chumash Indians—Social life and customs—
Juvenile literature. I. Title. II. We the people (Series) (Compass Point Books)
E99.C815R67 2005
979.4004'9758—dc22   2004018962

Copyright © 2005 by Compass Point Books
All rights reserved. No part of this book may be reproduced without written permission from the publisher. The publisher
takes no responsibility for the use of any of the materials or methods described in this book, nor for the products thereof.
Printed in the United States of America.

3065200166 3279

TABLE OF CONTENTS

A DESPERATE REVOLT

It was December 1823. In the sky above the mild, central coast of California, a comet flashed! Its blazing trail remained for days. Some of the suffering Chumash people there believed this was a sign from their ancient gods. It meant they soon would have better luck. This gave them courage in February 1824, when the largest Chumash revolt against the oppressive Spanish colonists began.

4

A comet with its long tail of dust

Spanish missionaries converted the Chumash, often by force.

For more than 50 years, Spanish priests of the Catholic religion had tried to convince the Chumash to become Christian. These missionaries demanded that the Chumash give up their own culture and their ways of believing and behaving. Many missionaries agreed with the words of one priest, who described native Californians as "savage, wild, and dirty." The missionaries believed

5

they were rescuing native people and saving their souls. Some missionaries spoke about Christian values. Some offered glass beads or food as "bait" to attract the Chumash.

More often, though, missionaries and the soldiers who helped them forced the Chumash people to live and work as Christians. All the while, the Chumash resisted. A visitor to one mission wrote about the Chumash being herded to church like cattle "under the whip's lash." By the winter of 1823–1824, beatings and cruel punishments were part of everyday life for Chumash who lived at Mission Santa Ynez, the nearby Mission La Purisima Concepcion, and Mission Santa Barbara.

In February 1824, however, the Chumash revolted. A soldier at Mission Santa Ynez had whipped a visiting Chumash from Mission La Purisima Concepcion. The Santa Ynez Chumash protested by setting fires and locking the missionaries into a small building. Soldiers arrived at Santa Ynez the next day to learn that these Chumash had fled to La Purisima Concepcion.

6

Native people paddle past a Spanish settlement built on their land.

At La Purisima Concepcion, a Chumash man named
Pacomio Poqui urged all the Chumash to continue to fight.
Written accounts from this time and stories told in Chumash
families describe what happened next. Some Chumash
remembered the comet. It even helped convince some
Chumash wise men that they could not be hurt. One said,
"If they shoot at me, the bullets will not enter my flesh."
Another said that only "water [would] come out of the cannon"
any soldiers fired. The Chumash then trapped missionaries
and soldiers in a storeroom. They also killed four visitors.

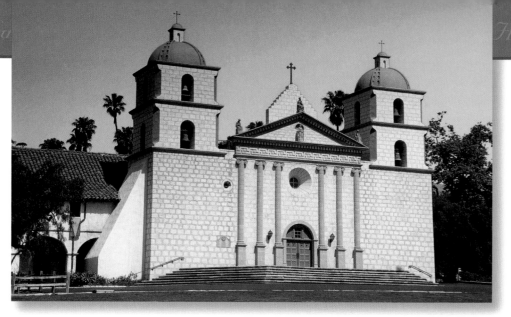

Mission Santa Barbara was established in 1786.

For a month, 400 Chumash ruled over La Purisima Concepcion. When 100 government soldiers arrived, however, their cannons quickly defeated the Chumash. Sixteen natives died. Pacomio Poqui was sentenced to 10 years in prison.

Meanwhile, the Chumash at Mission Santa Barbara had also revolted. They had more success. Led by Andres Sagimomatsse, about 500 Chumash overcame their guards and fled. Some remained free, but many were brought back. Many of those who escaped had to settle far to the east of their original homes to avoid being caught. This widespread, desperate revolt showed how much the Chumash missed their traditional way of life. They had lived that way for thousands of years.

THE "FIRST PEOPLE"

The Chumash (pronounced CHOO-mash) are a native people of the central California coast. About 10,000 years ago, their distant ancestors settled between what are the present-day cities of Paso Robles and Malibu. They also lived on the Northern Channel Islands just offshore. Slowly over time, these people developed the Chumash way of life. Ancient rock paintings created by the Chumash remind us of their life then.

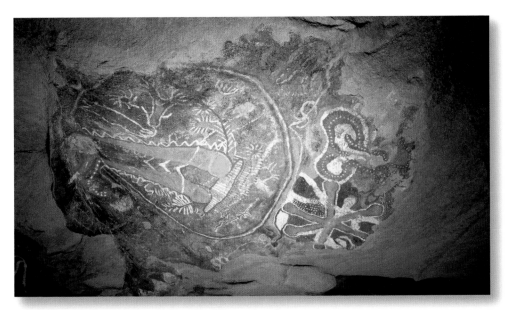

Rock paintings remain sacred to the Chumash today.

A map of Chumash lands

When the Spanish arrived in 1542, there were about 18,000 Chumash people who formed more than 150 communities. Their territory was roughly 7,000 square miles (18,200 square kilometers). The 2000 U.S. census lists only 4,032 Chumash people. Their original territory is also greatly reduced. The reservation of the Santa Ynez tribe of Chumash contains only 128 acres (51 hectares). About 150 Chumash live there. Most of the other Chumash live nearby in the California counties of Santa Barbara, San Luis Obispo, and Ventura.

In the past, there were at least eight Chumash divisions, and they all spoke languages related to one another. In their own languages, the Chumash called themselves the "First People" of their own villages.

The Chumash lived on the Channel Islands off California's coast.

The name "Chumash" sounds like their word for "bead money." Because Chumash living on the Channel Islands

11

made and used small seashell beads for money, mainland people may have begun calling these island dwellers the "bead money makers" or "Chumash." This name stuck and spread to all the Chumash.

Other tribes lived close to the Chumash. To the north, these included the Salinans and Yokuts. The Tataviam, Fernandeno, and Gabrielino peoples lived to the east and south. The generally peaceful Chumash traded with their neighbors. Sometimes, though, the Chumash fought over territory or for revenge.

12

PLEASANT SUMMERS AND GENTLE WINTERS

The coastal territory of the Chumash was so rich in food that they did not need to plant crops. Men fished and hunted in the ocean as well as in freshwater streams. They used clubs and harpoons to kill seals, otters, porpoises, and large fish. They used nets and hooks-and-lines to catch the many smaller fish. Clams and other seafood were also plentiful. Their meat provided food, and their shells made useful tools and jewelry.

The coastal area near Point Conception.

13

The Chumash ground acorns for cooking.

Women gathered acorns, other nuts, wild fruits, and roots. They cooked soups with ground acorns. Chumash men supplied the family with deer and smaller animals they hunted using spears and bows and arrows. These wooden spears and arrows often had sharpened stone or bone tips.

The Chumash home was a circle-shaped, round-topped house called an 'ap. It had a frame of bent willow poles and branches covered in overlapping layers of reeds. These reeds kept out the rain. Because of their mild climate, the Chumash usually cooked outdoors. However, the 'ap also had an indoor fire pit that could be used for cooking and heating. Smoke then escaped from a hole at the top of the 'ap. Otherwise, the top was covered by an animal skin.

14

With pleasant summers and gentle winters, the Chumash had little need for clothing. Women usually only wore knee-long skirts made of deerskin or woven bark strips or grass.

Sometimes Chumash women also wore caps woven like baskets. In the winter the caps kept their heads warm. Men only wore belts from which they strung tools. In winter, the Chumash sometimes added short, animal hide cloaks. A Chumash chief might wear a long bearskin cape to show his or her importance.

Reeds cover the poles and branches of a reconstructed 'ap.

VILLAGE LIFE

About 2,000 to 3,000 years ago, Chumash men began making large canoes called tomols. They cut driftwood or redwood into planks that were up to 2 feet (60 centimeters) long. They glued the planks together with pitch and tar. They tied the planks together with tough plant strings, and then decorated their finished boats. When they were completed, these large canoes were 20 to 30 feet (6 to 9 meters) long. In their sturdy canoes, the Chumash were able to fish in the ocean. They traveled along the coast and to and

Men today paddle a tomol, the traditional Chumash canoe.

from the Channel Islands to visit and trade. This important means of transportation influenced where the Chumash lived. They built permanent villages near creeks that ran into the sea. This way, they had not only a source of fresh water but an easy way to launch their tomols.

A Chumash sweat lodge is also called a temescal, a Spanish word derived from Aztec.

Chumash villages had between 200 and 1,000 residents. Besides 'aps, larger villages traditionally had other important buildings and spaces. The sweat lodge provided a place for men and, sometimes, women to clean themselves and make themselves pure. This building, called an 'apa'yik or *temescal,* was partly underground. It had mud covering its roof to keep in the heat of its special fire. Large villages also had storehouses, a dance

17

Rafael Solares, a Chumash wot, wears a traditional dance outfit in 1878.

The Chumash and Their History • The Chumash and Their History

ground for ceremonies, a playing field for games, and a nearby cemetery.

There was no one chief for all the Chumash. Each village had its own peacetime chief called a wot. Occasionally, one wot might govern two or three villages. This leader made important decisions and settled arguments. Usually, the position of wot passed from father to son, but women could inherit this job, too. A village wot lived in a larger 'ap than other Chumash. The wot might receive gifts from other villagers. Male chiefs also could have more than one wife.

During their rare wars, Chumash villagers followed a separate war captain. This leader was the bravest, boldest man in the village. He, too, lived in a larger 'ap and had more belongings than some villagers. Tomol owners were also highly regarded and usually wealthy.

DAILY LIFE

Two or more related Chumash families usually lived together in one 'ap. After a young couple married, they usually lived in the wife's village, near her mother. In addition, some belongings were inherited from a mother's family. For these reasons, even though the position of chief passed from father to son, a mother's family was very important. This family taught children the stories and customs of Chumash life.

A Chumash 'ap under construction

20

Their male relatives taught boys to fish, build 'aps, and hunt. Girls learned how to cook, care for children, and gather plants for food and medicine.

The Chumash also learned how to make the strong, beautiful baskets that they used daily. Chumash gathered, stored, and served food in these containers. Some of their baskets were

The Chumash have been making beautiful baskets for hundreds of years and exported them to other tribes.

coiled tightly enough to hold water and cook food in. Women dropped heated stones into water-filled baskets to boil food in them. The Chumash also kept valuable items and carried babies in baskets. Often, they used baskets as trade items with other peoples. These decorated baskets made of coiled or twined plant fibers were highly prized.

21

A playing field is set up for a game of shinny, which is similar to hockey.

The Chumash played as well as worked. On their large village playing fields, boys and men enjoyed hoop and pole games. Entire villages sometimes competed against each other in an action-packed ball and stick game like hockey. It was called tikauwich or shinny. The Chumash also enjoyed music and dance.

They sang and played flutes, whistles, and rattles. Some songs and dances were part of celebrations. The Chumash used a wooden clapper stick instead of a drum to beat the rhythm of their songs and dances.

Chumash villagers gathered together at special times of the year to enjoy themselves and honor the animals of their world. They wore special clothes and headdresses then that often included feathers and shells. One important ceremony honored the swordfish, and dancers wore headdresses made from the skulls of swordfish.

"WHILE THE SUN IS SHINING"

The Chumash worshipped the spirit of Mother Earth, whom they called Hutash. They said she had created all the creatures of this world. According to the Chumash, dolphins came into being when Hutash built a rainbow bridge between the Channel Islands and the mainland. Some Chumash fell off this bridge into the sea. Kind Hutash rescued them by turning them into dolphins.

Dolphins grace a fountain in Santa Barbara.

24

The sun sets along the California coast

The Chumash also worshipped the sun. They knew the rays of Father Sun made things grow. In mid winter, when days are the shortest, the Chumash held a special ceremony. They believed that these prayers, songs, and dances were needed at the winter solstice to bring back longer, sunlit days.

An elderly Chumash man named Kitsepawit remembered how these beliefs were used to teach good behavior. Kitsepawit was told to "never do anything [bad] and think that no one will see you. For while the sun is shining, an eye is here. ... [I]f a man [acted like the sun] ... [h]e would have noble feelings to help his neighbors."

In each village, a group of religious leaders called 'antap was responsible for important ceremonies. The 'antap helped keep the forces of nature in balance. They also took part in dances that honored creatures such as the swordfish, bear, and coyote. The Chumash told many stories about how these creatures were part of the world. For the Chumash, these stories held sacred truth.

The Chumash had special healers called shamans. The shamans were both respected and feared for their knowledge of the spirit world. The Chumash thought a shaman could cure illness. They believed he or she used secret knowledge along with plants for these cures. The Chumash also believed some shamans could tell the future and explain the meanings of dreams. A shaman supposedly communicated directly with the spirits.

People who study the Chumash marvel at the colorful paintings they left inside caves and other hidden, rocky places. Shamans may have made these paintings as one way to pray to the spirits. The circles, stars, and animal and people shapes of the paintings may have had special religious meanings for the

A museum exhibit depicts a Chumash shaman painting a dream vision.

Chumash. People who study the Chumash think some Chumash cave paintings show the positions of stars and constellations. They think that shamans used these positions to determine the winter solstice and other dates for important ceremonies.

27

WHITE MEN'S WAYS

In 1542, Juan Rodriguez Cabrillo, a Portuguese explorer in the service of Spain, met the Chumash. He and his sailors were searching for good land for a Spanish colony. The gentle climate of Chumash territory seemed perfect. The Chumash were also friendly and eager to trade with these newcomers. Yet this meeting had terrible results for the Chumash.

Juan Rodriguez Cabrillo died on January 3, 1543, from complications of a broken leg after a skirmish with native people.

28

By 1772, priests of the Catholic religion, led by Father Junipero Serra, began to settle in the area. They built the mission of San Luis Obispo. These missionaries wanted to help the Chumash by converting them to Christianity and white men's ways. The five missions established in the area, though, brought pain, disease, and death to the Chumash.

A statue of Father Junipero Serra stands in San Francisco's Golden Gate Park.

In addition to the mission at San Luis Obispo, missions named Santa Barbara, San Buenaventura, La Purisima Concepcion, and Santa Ynez were later built in Chumash territory. Chumash workers helped priests build these missions. The converts were then kept at the missions. They farmed and did other work that also supplied soldiers and colonists farther away.

29

Many priests did not respect or understand the Chumash way of life. They saw Chumash ceremonies as devil worship and did not believe that they could hold any values equal to Christianity. Father Geronimo Boscana wrote that a typical California native had eyes that "are never uplifted, but like those of the swine, are cast to the earth. Truth is not in him."

The Chumash were forced to learn about Christianity.

Such beliefs influenced how the missionaries treated the Chumash. They locked up or beat the native people who did not work according to a mission schedule. Chumash who ran away were brought back and cruelly punished by soldiers. In addition to beatings, these run-aways might be made to work while wearing heavy metal chains or wooden shoes. Sometimes, Chumash who broke rules were starved for days. Native workers suffered in another way. Many converts caught diseases carried by the Spanish. Because the Chumash had no immunity to these illnesses, many died. In 1806, hundreds of Chumash died in a measles epidemic.

In 1821, Mexico won its independence from Spain. The new country of Mexico now governed Chumash territory. However, this change did not help the Chumash. They continued to suffer from disease, overwork, and other cruel treatment. This led to the failed Chumash revolt of 1824.

In the 1830s, the Mexican government began to sell or give away Chumash land to settlers. Fewer than 3,000 Chumash were left alive by then. Some Chumash found work as servants or cowboys on ranches. Others moved away from their traditional territory to start new villages inland. By

Mexican governor Pío Pico sold 15 of the 21 California missions to ranchers in 1845.

1839, one official counted only 246 Chumash left in the Santa Barbara area. Thousands of Chumash had lived there when the Spanish first arrived.

WORKING AS SLAVES

In 1848, the United States won a two-year war with Mexico and now governed Chumash land. This change did not help the Chumash either. When gold was discovered in California, settlers had a new reason to want traditional native land. Then in 1850, the territory of California officially became the 31st state. Once this occurred, more white settlers arrived to take over land that Chumash had lived on for thousands of years.

The discovery of gold brought many settlers to California.

State and federal laws did not protect or help the Chumash. One California law even declared, "In no case shall a white man be convicted of any offense upon the testimony of an Indian." On the other hand, the word of any white person was enough to have a native person declared a "vagrant" and, therefore, sentenced to up to four months of unpaid labor.

A historical photo of a Chumash child and two women was taken in Ventura.

Chumash and other native children were at special risk under these new laws. If a relative supposedly approved and received a one-time payment, children could be made to work until they were legal adults. The children themselves then got no payment other than their food and clothing. They worked as slaves.

34

The Chumash received land near Santa Ynez Mission in 1901.

One California landowner of this time thought that such child workers were a good investment. He said that "Indians of seven or eight years old are worth $100." Most often, native children worked at household chores, cooking, and caring for babies.

By 1880, records show that there were only about 300 Chumash people left alive. In 1901, a small part of their traditional territory was returned to them at last.

The U.S. government gave them land near Santa Ynez Mission, where many Chumash had once lived. This area was officially declared the Santa Ynez Reservation.

By then, however, few Chumash who remembered traditional ways were left. One was the elderly man named Kitsepawit, also known by the Spanish name of Fernando Librado. Kitsepawit spoke with John Harrington, an anthropologist who studied the Chumash. He explained how his people had built tomols. Before he died in 1915, Kitsepawit told Harrington about many other Chumash customs and languages. Maria Solares was another elderly Chumash who helped record her people's customs.

"PROUD OF WHO THEY ARE"

Today, the small Santa Ynez tribe of Chumash governs its own reservation. It has a constitution and elects officials and a tribal chairperson. They deal with county, state, and federal matters affecting the Santa Ynez people. A business council runs a casino that provides income for tribe members.

The American and Chumash flags fly at the tribal office.

37

Members of the Chumash Maritime Association participate
in a tomol crossing to the Channel Islands.

Most Chumash peoples, though, are still seeking federal recognition as tribes. These include the Coastal, the Barbareno, the San Luis Obispo, the Island, the Purisimeno, and the Ventura Chumash. Several of these modern Chumash groups get their names from the Spanish missions near where their ancestors lived. Federal recognition would help today's Chumash regain some of their traditional land as reservations.

Today, Chumash people like other members of modern society hold jobs, attend schools, shop at stores, watch TV, and play games. Many Chumash speak

Spanish as well as English. Yet the Chumash are proud of their past. They wish to preserve their traditions.

Chumash storytellers keep their ancient stories alive. Some Chumash are learning one of their original languages, still officially considered extinct. The University of California helps them. While many Chumash are Christian, some Chumash practice their traditional religion. Some Christian Chumash honor their past by participating in cere- monies such as the Swordfish Dance.

A Chumash storyteller preserves the ancient stories of her ancestors.

Many Chumash people today work together to preserve their history and values. As James Leon of the Kern County Chumash Council says, his people are uniting so their "children can be proud of who they are and where they came from." Chumash groups have protested the building of an energy plant at Point Conception. The Chumash consider this coastal area sacred. The Chumash are also concerned about people digging up their cemeteries and harming rock paintings. Some of these holy native places are still in danger, though laws passed in the 1970s and 1980s do protect some sacred spots.

The Chumash have a long history of respect for Earth and its creatures. In the future, they hope to continue this tradition as they regain stolen customs and rights.

An archaeologist brings an ancient Chumash bowl to the ocean surface near the Channel Islands. Groups are working together to preserve the past.

41

GLOSSARY

casino—an establishment for legal gambling

census—an official government count of the number of people in certain groups

comet—piece of ice and rock that has a long tail of dust and orbits the sun

converting—convincing a person or people to change their religion to another one

epidemic—a widespread disease affecting many people

immunity—the ability of the body to resist a disease

mission—a place where people live and teach their religious beliefs

pitch—a sticky substance made from pine sap

solstice—either of two times of the year when the sun is farthest from the equator; the summer solstice is the longest day of the year and the winter solstice is the shortest

vagrant—someone without a regular home or job

DID YOU KNOW?

- The Chumash used pelican, condor, and eagle feathers in their fancy headdresses for religious ceremonies.

- Some California communities such as Lompoc and Malibu get their names from the Chumash language.

- In addition to the five missions on traditional Chumash land, there were 16 other missions along 650 miles (1,040 kilometers) of the California coast.

- The last Chumash tomols actually used for fishing were made around 1850.

IMPORTANT DATES

Timeline

10,000 B.C.	Distant ancestors of Chumash settle along California coast.
1542	Explorer Juan Rodriguez Cabrillo meets the Chumash.
1772	Mission San Luis Obispo, the first of five, is built in Chumash area.
1806	Hundreds of Chumash die in a measles epidemic.
1821	Mexico becomes independent of Spain and then governs the Chumash.
1824	Chumash revolt at three missions.
1848	United States wins a war with Mexico and then governs California.
1850	California becomes a state, and more white settlers take Chumash land.
1901	Some Chumash get the Santa Ynez Reservation.
1970s	Laws passed through the 1980s protect some Chumash sacred places.

IMPORTANT PEOPLE

JUAN RODRIGUEZ CABRILLO (? –1543)
Portuguese explorer in the service of Spain who first met the Chumash

JOHN P. HARRINGTON (1884–1961)
Anthropologist and linguist who studied the Chumash

KITSEPAWIT (FERNANDO LIBRADO) (1839–1915)
Elderly Chumash man who preserved his people's traditions and described their history and ways to John P. Harrington

PACOMIO POQUI (1794–1844)
Chumash man who led the 1824 revolt at Mission Santa Ynez

ANDRES SAGIMOMATSSE (1768–1828)
Chumash man who led the 1824 revolt at Mission Santa Barbara

FATHER JUNIPERO SERRA (1713–1784)
Franciscan priest who arrived in California in 1769 to start missions; his work in Chumash territory began in 1772

MARIA SOLARES (1840s–1923)
Elderly Chumash woman who spoke with John Harrington about her people's customs and beliefs

45

WANT TO KNOW MORE?

At the Library

Anderson, Dale. *The California Missions.* Milwaukee, Wis.: World Almanac, 2002.

Behrens, June. *Missions of the Central Coast.* Minneapolis: Lerner, 1996.

Bial, Raymond. *The Chumash.* New York: Benchmark Books, 2004.

McCall, Lynne, and Rosalind Perry. *California's Chumash Indians.* San Luis
Obispo, Calif.: EZ Nature Books, 2002

On the Web

For more information on the *Chumash,* use FactHound to track
down Web sites related to this book.

1. Go to *www.facthound.com*

2. Type in a search word related to this book
   or this book ID: 0756508355.

3. Click on the *Fetch It* button.

Your trusty FactHound will fetch the best Web sites for you!

On the Road

Painted Cave State Historic Park

Highway 154 and San Marcos Road

Santa Barbara, CA

805/733-3713

To see a cave filled with Chumash rock paintings

Chumash Interpretive Center

3290 Lang Ranch Parkway

Thousand Oaks, CA

805/492-8076

To see a re-created Chumash village and a cave with rock paintings

Look for more We the People books about this era:

The Alamo

The Arapaho and Their History

The Battle of the Little Bighorn

The Buffalo Soldiers

The California Gold Rush

The Creek and Their History

The Erie Canal

Great Women of the Old West

The Lewis and Clark Expedition

The Louisiana Purchase

The Mexican War

The Ojibwe and Their History

The Oregon Trail

The Pony Express

The Santa Fe Trail

The Transcontinental Railroad

The Trail of Tears

The Wampanoag and Their History

The War of 1812

A complete list of We the People titles is available on our Web site:
www.compasspointbooks.com

INDEX

About the Author

Natalie M. Rosinsky writes about history, social studies, economics, science, and other fun things. One of her two cats usually sits on her computer as she works in Mankato, Minnesota. Natalie earned graduate degrees from the University of Wisconsin and has been a high school and college teacher.